The Visions of Nostradamus

A Magic Eye Book

by N.E. Thing Enterprises

Andrews and McMeel
A Universal Press Syndicate Company
Kansas City

ISBN: 0-8362-7056-8

Special thanks to the gifted hands of our art staff: Bohdan Petyhyrycz, Peter Ciavarella, Cheri Smith, and Andy Paraskevas.

Tom Baccei, President
N.E. Thing Enterprises

FOREWORD

As we mapped out the life of Michel de Nostredame during the filming of *Nostradamus,* it became clear that, although this was a man who lived 400 years ago, his writings and experiences have a devastating relevance to modern times.

As a medical student in sixteenth-century France, Nostradamus incurred the wrath of the authorities by treating the plague with herbalism. The battle between traditional and alternative medicine continues today. His knowledge of spiritual writings was greatly feared and forbidden by the Church, but inspired admiration and support from Queen Catherine. Today, in our highly stressful lives, the search for ancient religions and beliefs, yoga, astrology, etc., to gain some relief continues and these devices, once accepted, are now gaining more and more credibility. Indeed, Tcheky Karyo, who plays Nostradamus in the film, embarked on an intensive training in yoga and meditation in order to prepare for this exhausting role.

However, it was the visions of Michel de Nostrademe that made the most impact upon the cast and crew of *Nostradamus.* When I flew to Los Angeles with the first print of the film, it was the day on which the earthquake took place there in January 1994—accurately predicted by Nostradamus, and depicted in the opening scene of the film.

During this time, the books of Magic Eye images were gaining in popularity, and once more the resonance between Nostradamus and modern times became obvious. Through the computer-generated images of Magic Eye, we could experience the visions of Nostradamus for ourselves.

Nostradamus's foretelling of the French Revolution in 1789, the rise of Hitler, and the assassination of President Kennedy is well known, but it occurred to us that by choosing fifteen of Nostradamus's future prophecies, it would be possible for us all to, literally, see into the future.

We scanned the books of Nostradamus for prophecies that would have a universal appeal and relevance, and found that, although these prophecies were written four hundred years ago, most are credible and some contain accurate references to personalities and situations peculiar only to modern times. Thus, you can see aliens on television, cures for cancer and AIDS (the plague of the twentieth century), and, to give hope to us all, the dawning of a Golden Age.

As an added bonus, we have put date images beneath the coded writings of Nostradamus. Through use of your Magic Eye, you might be able to see into the future, but can you decipher the date image and accurately pinpoint when these prophecies are to take place?

So, no herbs or medication required, but with the help of Magic Eye, put yourself into Nostradamus's shoes and look into the future.

Edward Simons
Producer of the film *Nostradamus*

To Annie-T, for love and support

For nine years the reign of the slim thing will continue
then it will fall into so bloody a thirst
that a great lawless nation will die because of it:
killed by a better-natured man.

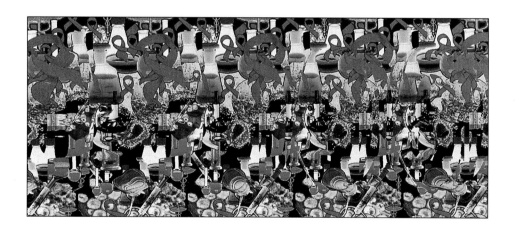

3

Earth-shaking fire from the center of the Earth
will cause trembling around a new city.
Two great rocks will make war for a long time.
Then Arethusa will redden in a new river.

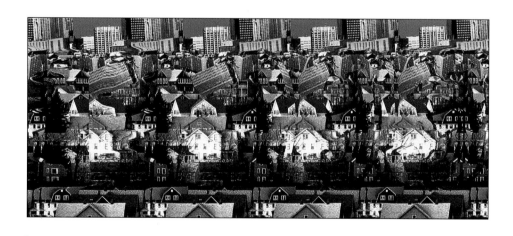

On a road someone televises intelligent aliens from the sky
with a broken, limping appearance.
He (or she) will put them into flight.
He sends them home, although here they alter belief.

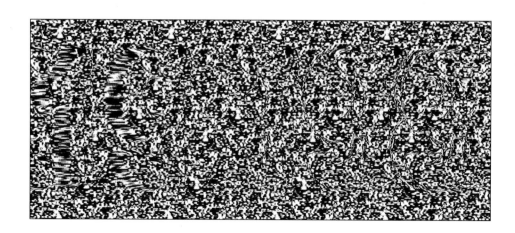

Mars known.
A journey to the planet near to the great age.
A new power that grows instead of lessens.
A staggering success. Possession outside the rocket.

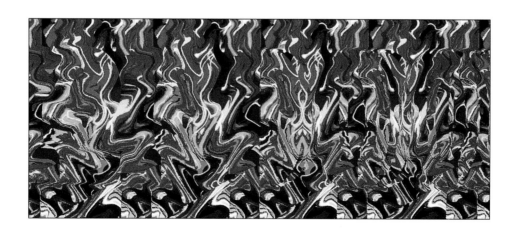

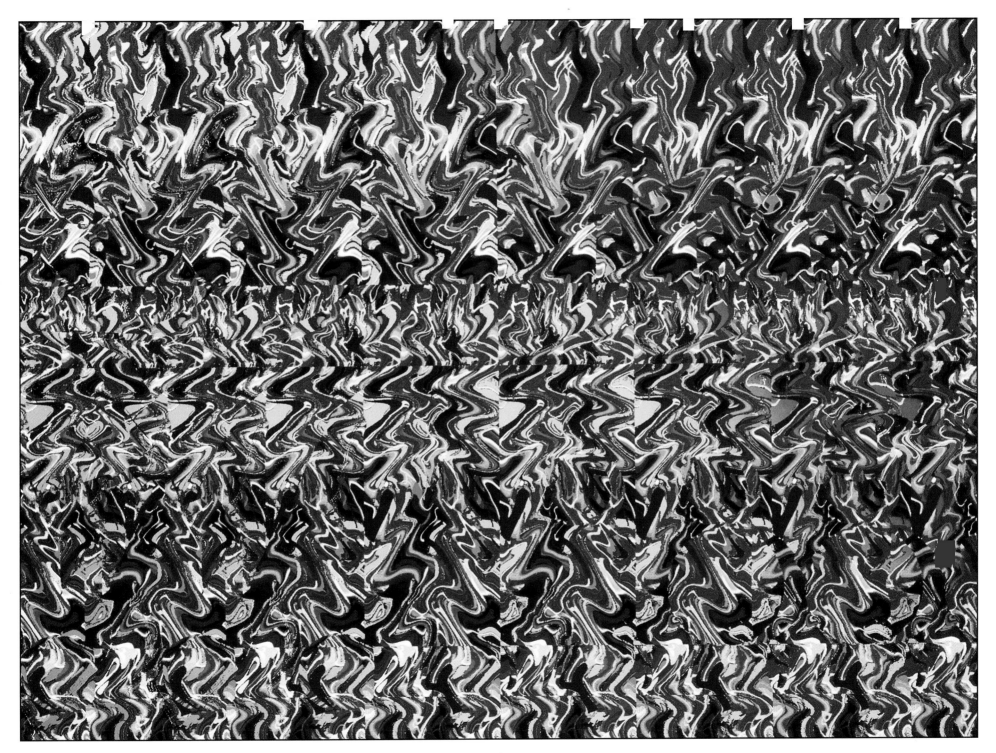

9

One day the two great masters will become friends.

Their great power will be seen to increase.

The new land (America) will be at the height of its power.

To the man of blood, the number will be reported.

The two will not remain united long:

within thirteen years they face barbarian power.

There will be such loss on both sides

that one will bless the barque of (St. Peter) and his cape.

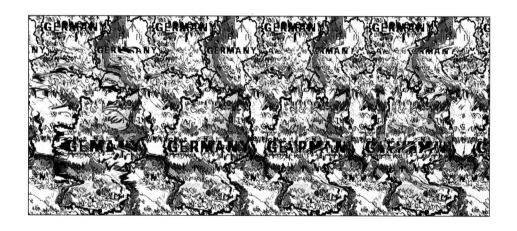

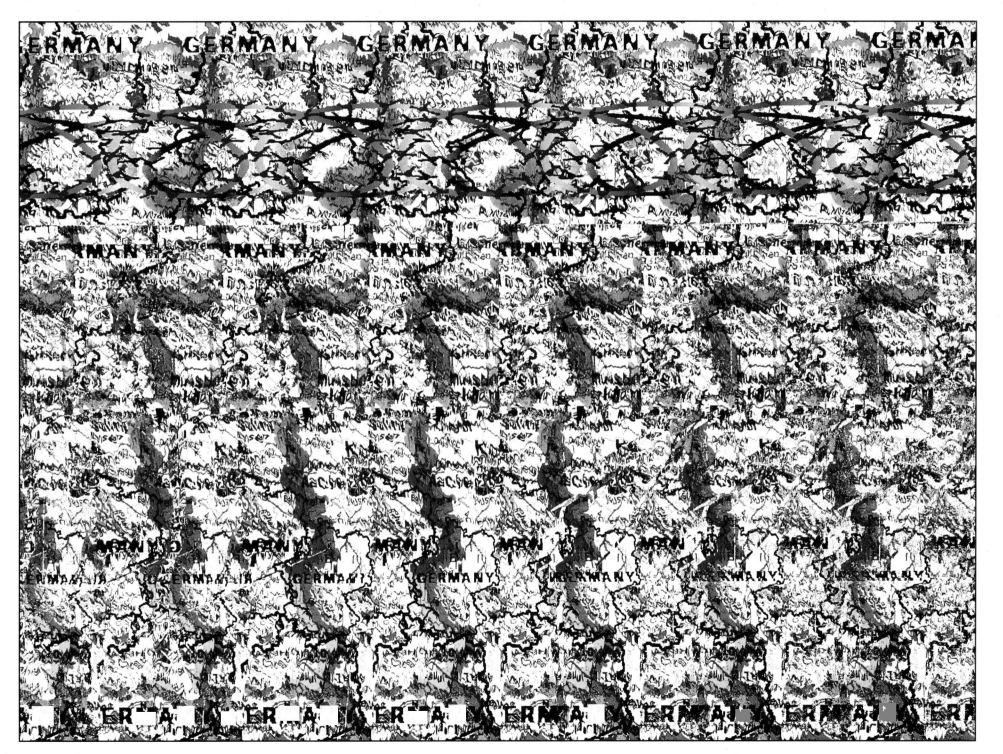

In half Baja (California) a great deluge falls and thunders soon,
enormous waves from the Gulf of California
break upon the shores of Mexico.
They reach as far as steeped Sonora.

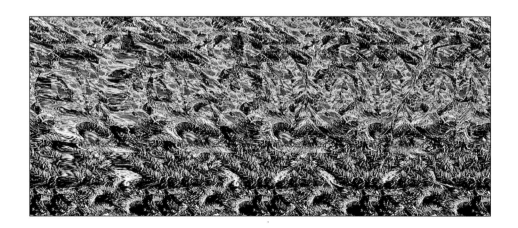

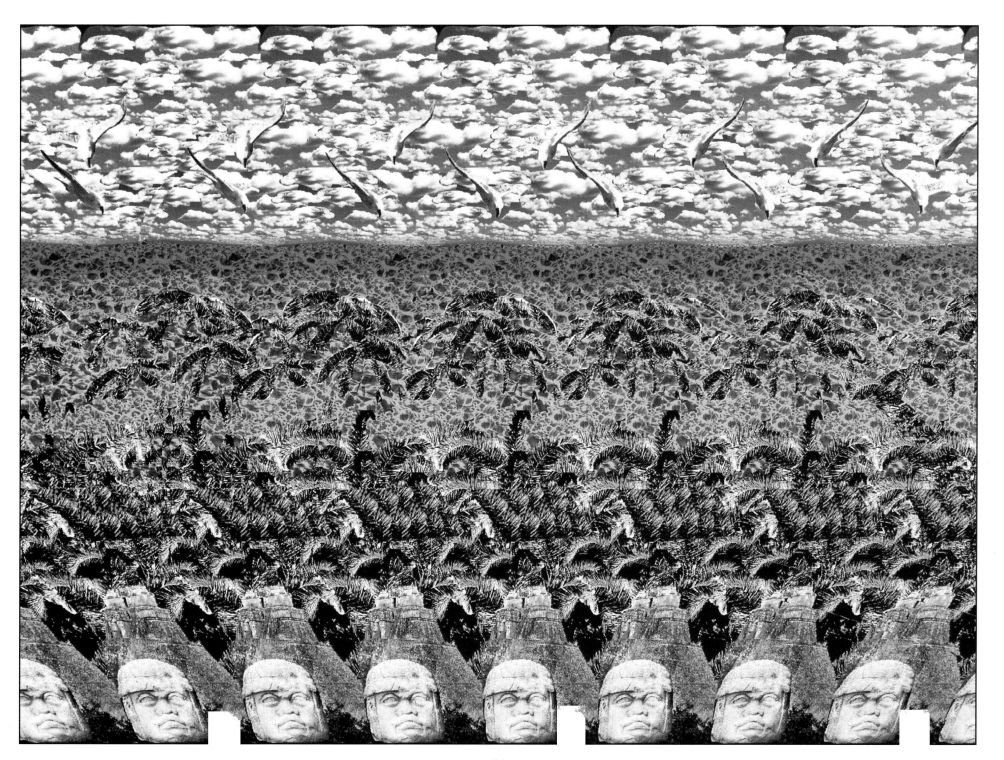

The royal scepter will have to accept that which
his predecessors have employed.
Because they do not understand the ring when
they come to destroy the palace.

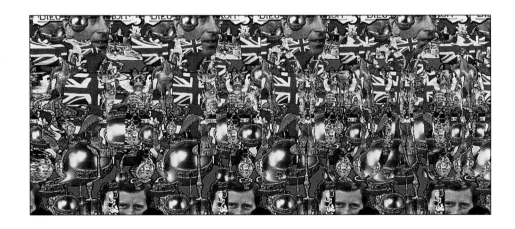

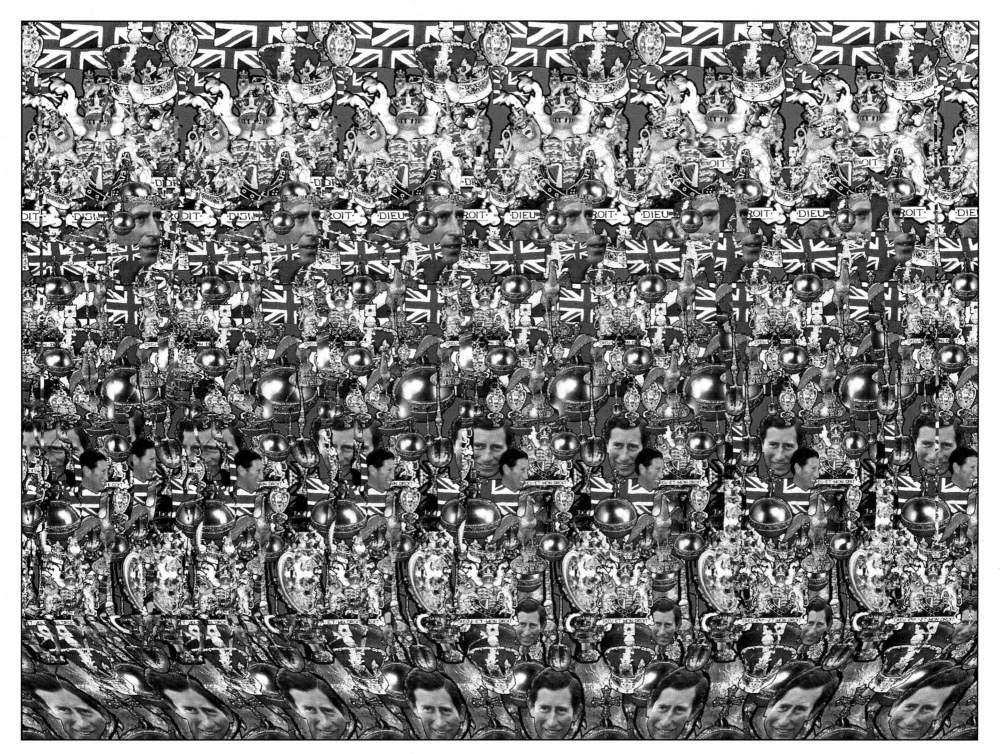

For according to the celestial sign, the Golden Age shall return,
and after all calculations, with the world near to
an all-encompassing revolution . . .
This will be after the visible judgment of heaven
before we reach the millennium,
which shall complete all.

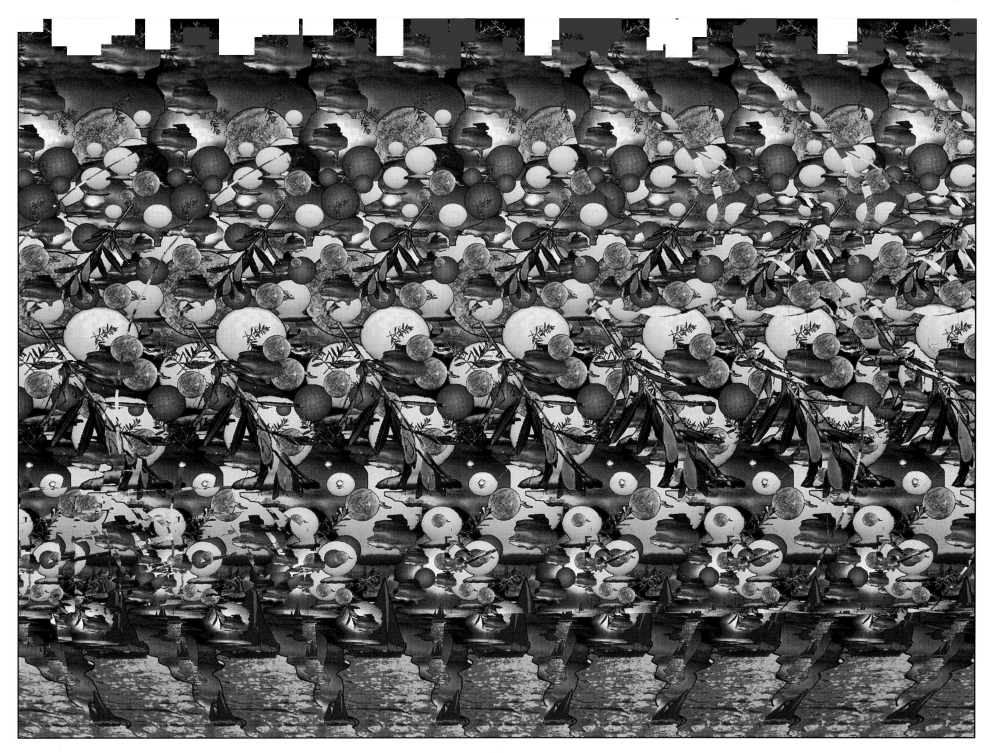

A Russian spacecraft will crash on America.
Two people killed.
The leader Yeltsin will hardly listen to the acrimony.
A fool shown up by bloodshed.

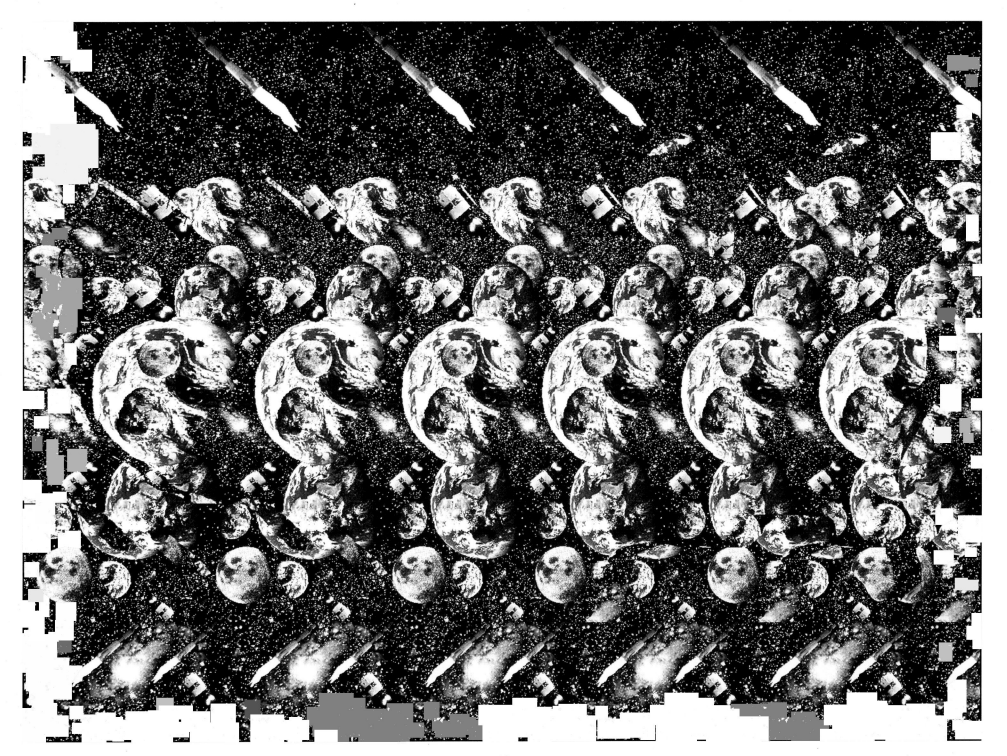

After assessment gives the unique frequency
to operate on the patients, waves of sound kill the cancers.
They become lifeless.
Their poisons leave the body.

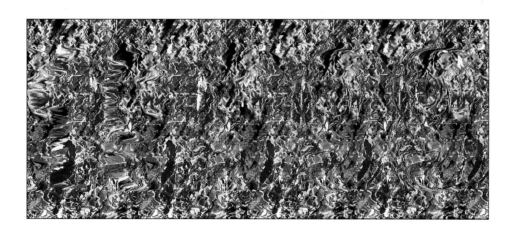

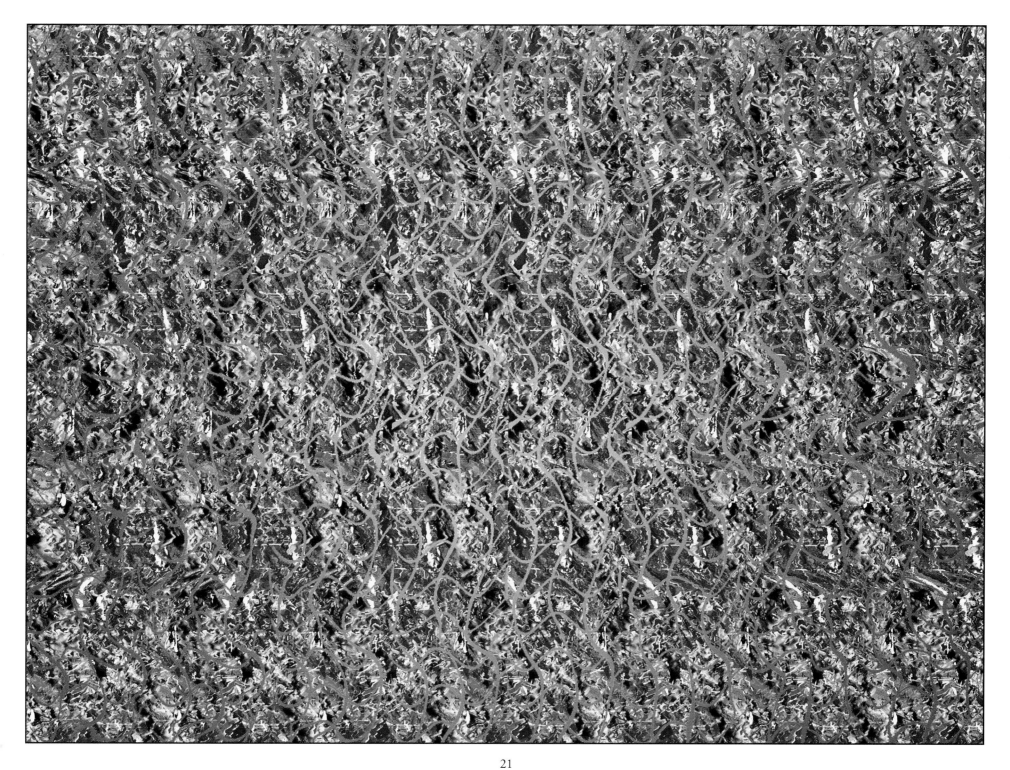

New medical treatments for the disease of aging,
the old grown young with smooth skin.
The senile lose their confusion. Robotic luxury.
A pure rhythm kicks at lumps.

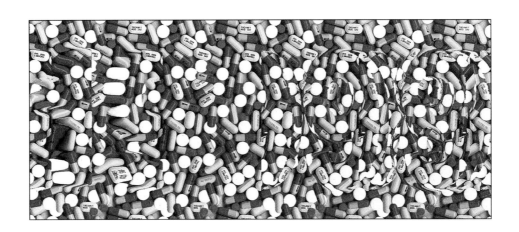

There will be omens in the spring and extraordinary changes thereafter,
reversals of nations and mighty earthquakes.
And there shall be in the month of October a great movement of the globe,
and it will be such that that one will think the Earth
has lost its gravitational movement
and that it will be plunged into the abyss of perpetual darkness.

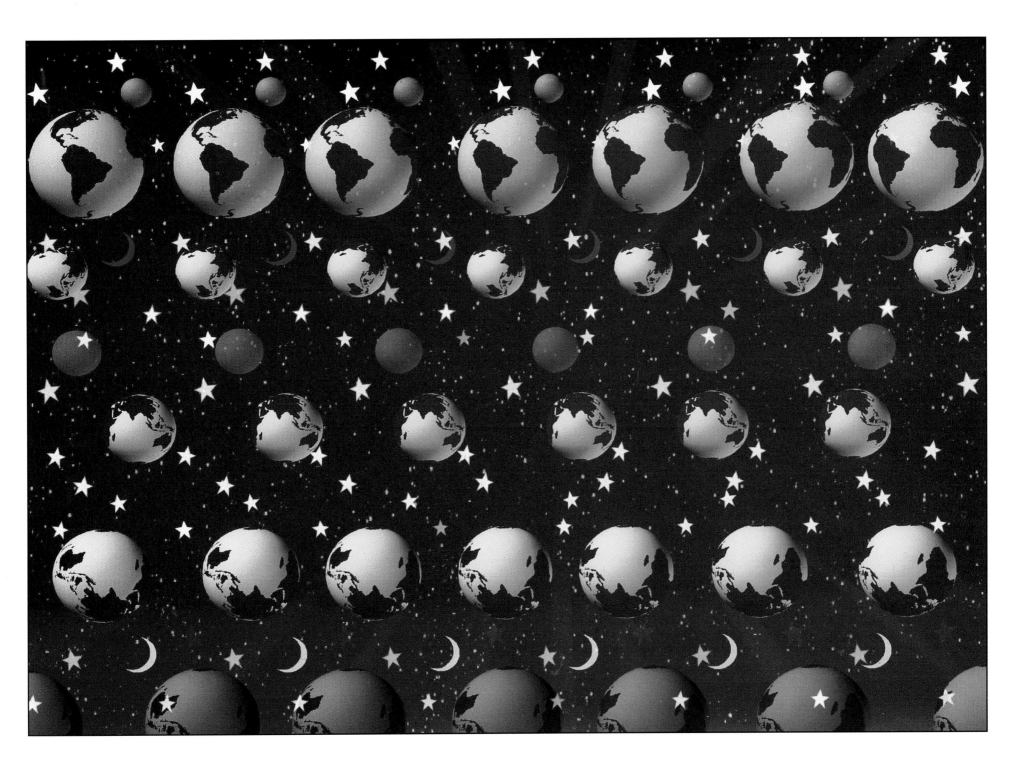

After a great muster of men (soldiers), another, bigger one is being prepared; God will renew the ages. Revolution and bloodshed will bring famine, war, and pestilence; then fire will be seen in the sky and a great rocket traversing it.

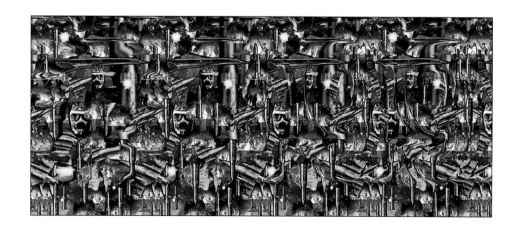

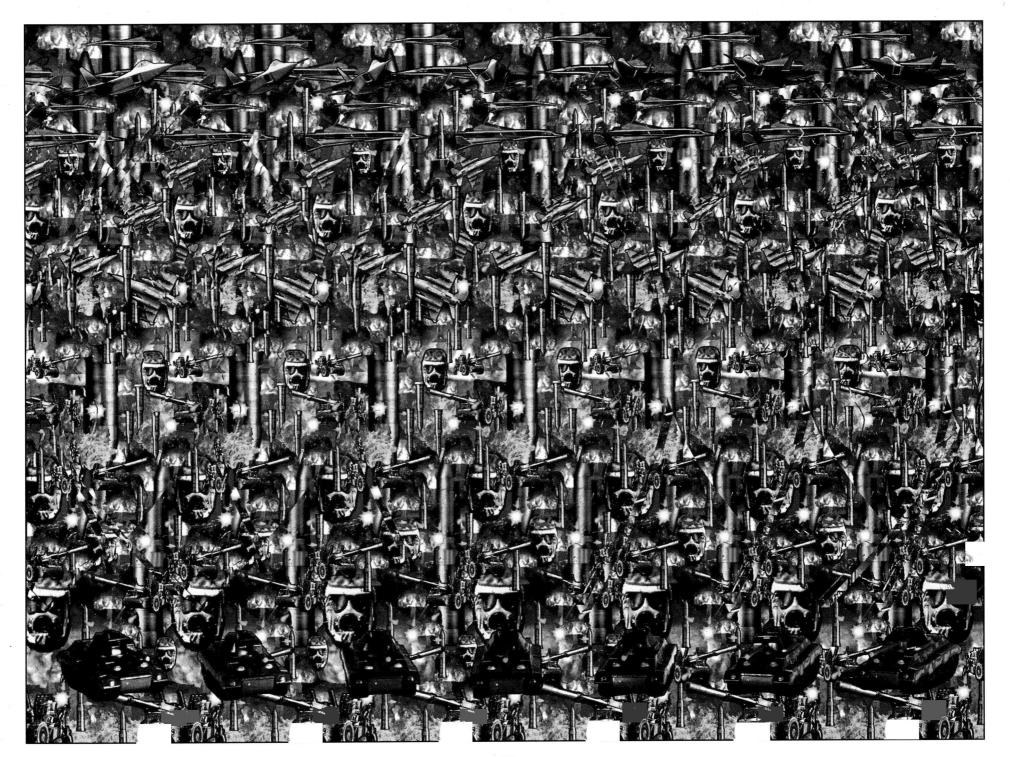

Not from Spain, but from ancient France
one will be elected for the trembling ship,
to the enemy will make promise
who in this reign will cause a terrible plague.

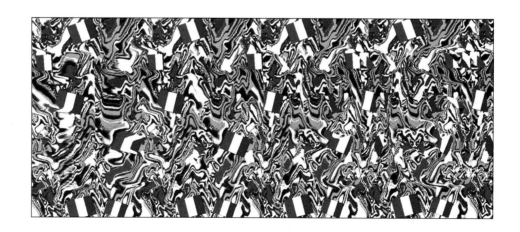

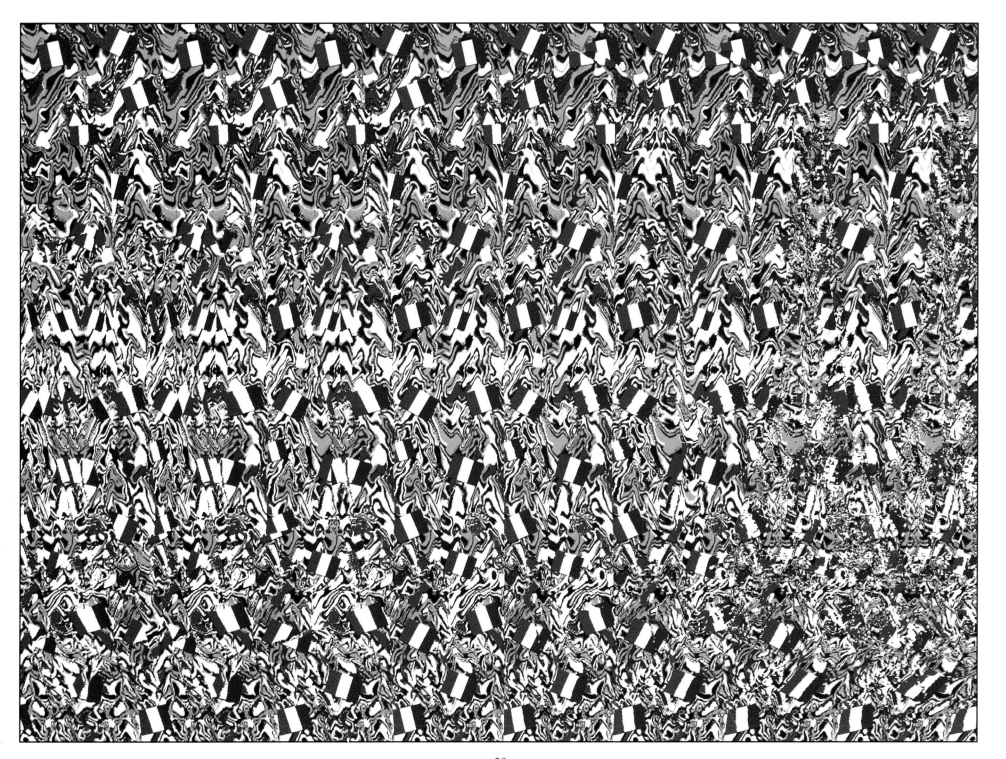

29

In places and times of flesh given fish (or fish meat),
the law of the commune will be made contrary:
it will remain strong for the old ones, then removed from the center,
the loving of everything in common put far behind.

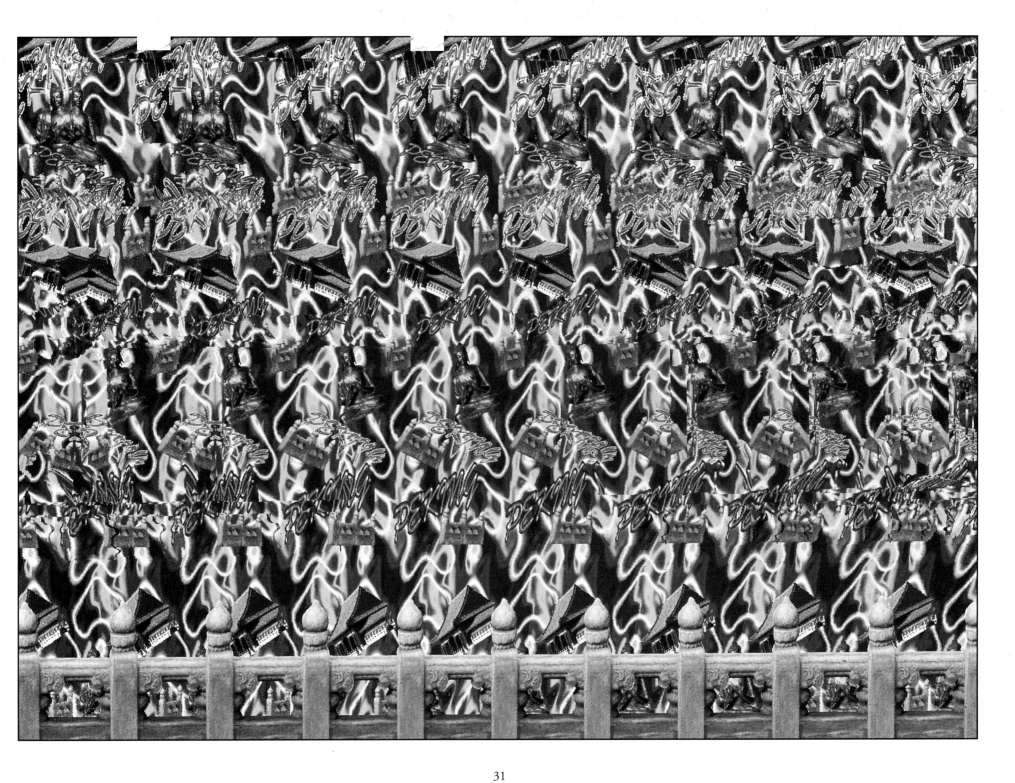

31

p. 3   A Cure for AIDS

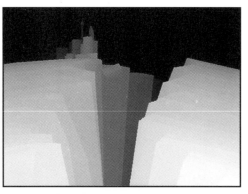

p. 5   Massive Earthquake
and Tidal Wave

p. 7   Aliens Televised

p. 9   Mission to Mars

p. 11   Return of the Cold War

p. 13   Giant Waves Hit Mexico

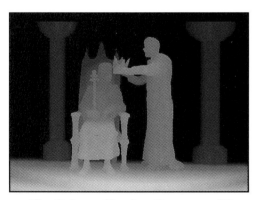

p. 15   Prince Charles Becomes King

p. 17   Beginning of the Golden Age

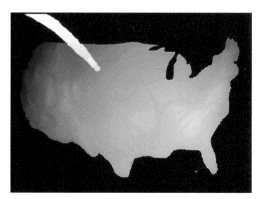

p. 19   Spacecraft Crashed
on America

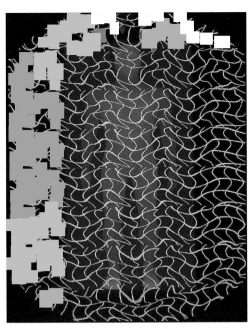

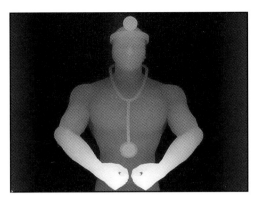

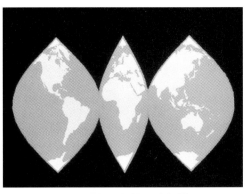